DECADE OF
DESTINY

DECADE OF DESTINY

GEORGE E. VANDEMAN

Pacific Press Publishing Association
Boise, Idaho
Oshawa, Ontario, Canada

Edited by Bonnie Widicker
Designed by Tim Larson
Cover photo by Ellen Schuster/Image Bank©
Typeset in 11/12 Century Schoolbook

Author assumes full responsibility for all facts and
quotations cited in this book.

Unless otherwise indicated, Scripture references in
this book are from the New King James Version.

**Library of Congress Catalog Card Number: 89-
62800**

ISBN 0-8163-1879-9

89 90 91 92 93 • 5 4 3 2 1

Contents

Chapter 1

Decade of Destiny

A hundred years ago, life for most Americans seemed happy and carefree. The Gay Nineties they called it. Excitement and optimism pervaded the land, from the bustling harbors of New York to the blossoming orchards of California.

And why not be upbeat? The West had been won. Our nation had recovered from its Civil War. The Industrial Revolution promised a peaceful and prosperous utopia. No wonder the future sparkled with star-spangled possibilities.

Unfortunately, how times have changed from those "Gay Nineties"! A century later, the word *gay* itself no longer means happy and carefree living. Now it connotes controversy, pain, and deadly disease. In many other ways we've also suffered serious loss in our society, despite all our technological advances. Many thoughtful observers see this time in earth's history as the Decade of Destiny—our "make it or break it" moment of truth with human survival hanging in the balance.

Having so much at stake, it seems fitting for us in this book to investigate the explosive issues of our time. Only then can we be informed and prepared for whatever lies ahead. We will find in the Scriptures surprisingly relevant solutions for society's perplexing problems.

Problem solving was far from the minds of many Americans in the 1890s. Back then, it seemed that the world was getting better and better. The *New York Times* typified the spirit of the day when it proclaimed in an editorial: "We step upon the threshold of . . . the new century, facing a still brighter dawn of civilization."

The nation was at peace overseas, while at home, Civil War wounds had healed. Although racism remained, at least the country had rid itself of the cancer of slavery. Economic prosperity fueled the industrial revolution, accelerated by new transcontinental railroads.

Scientific breakthroughs unleashed a startling stream of new discoveries such as the X-ray, which revolutionized surgery. Tractors promised to give farmers a new lease on life. Electricity offered untold wonders—someone had even invented a toaster!

Best of all was the motorcar. In 1892 William Morrison paraded the first automobile through the streets of Chicago. At the end of the decade, nearly 8,000 cars sputtered their way around the country.

The new invention did pose some problems. One writer explained, "The operator [of a motorcar] must combine the intelligence of the driver with that of the horse." Prudently, New York City enforced a speed limit of nine miles per hour.

Life was simpler back in the 1890s. Even our government in Washington wasn't as complex as it is today. White House correspondent Albert Halstead observed, "It is not always necessary, although better, to make an engagement [an appointment] to see the president." Well, that certainly has changed now!

In New York Harbor, the Statue of Liberty opened her arms to a better life for millions of immigrants passing through Ellis Island. Wages were low a century ago, but prices were low too. A Chicago couple furnishing a home could buy a mahogany parlor table for $3.95, a sofa for $9.98, and a brass-trimmed bed for $3.00. Top quality suits cost $10.65; shirts, 23 cents.

In the 1890s, steelmaster Andrew Carnagie saw his annual profits double. There seemed no limit for someone with talent and ambition. Horatio Alger fueled the fantasies of millions when he suggested: "If you are good and work hard, someday you will be rich." Even farmers enjoyed the prosperity of bumper crops.

There were challenges, of course—plenty of them. As I mentioned, racism persisted, not to be dealt with until decades later when the social patriot Martin Luther King, Jr., called us to moral accountability. While the nineteenth century American economy soared during the Industrial Revolution, too many factories were sweatshops, where women and even children endured long hours in danger and drudgery for a pittance—$3.54 a week—while wealthy industrialists pocketed the profits.

All things considered, though, life was looking up. The Chicago World's Exposition showcased the spirit of the 1890s. Scientific progress and a love for entertainment combined in the graceful Ferris Wheel—but there was nothing scientific about the dancer "Little Egypt," a forerunner of the unabashed hedonism in the Roaring Twenties.

In the 1890s, secular humanism flourished—the belief that we humans have within ourselves the resources needed to survive and thrive. Darwin's evolutionary theory was gaining ground; even ministers got swept up in heralding an evolving utopia. In the words of one pastor:

> Laws are becoming more just, rulers humane; music is becoming sweeter and books wiser; homes are happier, and the individual heart becoming at once more just and more gentle.

Sounds a lot like the kinder, gentler nation we are still longing for today. Since the 1890s we have suffered two world wars and continual conflict of all kinds. Of course, our labor situation has dramatically improved, and much progress has been made in civil rights. But despite America's economic and social achievement, we find ourselves in a more precarious situation than ever before.

Consider the economy. Business may still be thriving on the coasts, but our heartland has been suffering. Farms, mines, oil fields, and steel mills have languished, leaving thousands unemployed. Homeless families haunt the streets of our cities—and rural areas too. Worse yet, tidings of economic trouble brewing overseas may be more threatening than any domestic devastation. Nearly 2,000 years ago, the apostle James penned a startling warning of hard times in the time of the end:

> Come now, you rich, weep and howl for your miseries that are coming upon you! Your riches are corrupted, and your garments are moth-eaten. Your gold and silver are corroded (James 5:1-3).

Here we have a dismal portrayal of world finances in the last days. Just when the wealthy are enjoying economic prosperity, business as usual, something unsettling happens. Our financial system disintegrates to the point that wealth is "corroded"—symbolizing severe economic crisis.

Who could forget Black Monday, October 19, 1987? Amid the frenzied shouting of Wall Street traders, the market plummeted more than 500 points in one terrifying day, plunging even deeper, percentage-wise, than any single day of the Great Depression. Although our economy rallied, we saw chilling evidence that what some experts said could never happen did happen, like a bolt out of the blue sky.

And, according to the Scripture we just read, an economic collapse is indeed on its way. When our monetary structure crumbles, a time of trouble results, described in the passage we just read as a "day of slaughter." And God's Word predicted all this would happen just before the "coming of the Lord"—the time in which you and I live today.

As we contemplate the financial crisis approaching, let me assure you of this. You can be safe and secure even during any economic collapse. Safe in God's care—provided you are willing to accept His conditions.

Back in the 1890s, America stood proudly at the height of military strength. The easily-won Spanish-American War planted the Stars and Stripes on the shores of Asia. The United States had arrived as an unchallenged world power. But beyond the horizon, trouble loomed. As the nineteenth century faded, Kaiser Wilhelm in Berlin fired thirty-three guns to salute a new era for Germany, to "win the place she had not attained," as he put it. The horrors of World War I followed, after which came an even more devastating World War II. Without question, our world could not survive another all-out war.

Come with me back to October 1962, those spine-tingling days of the Cuban missile crisis. Khrushchev, the cagey old dictator, dared to test the resolve of our forceful young president, John Kennedy. We edged perilously close to nuclear war—much closer than previously known, recently declassified records reveal. Thank God, the Soviets backed down and granted the world a stay of execution.

In recent years, with both superpowers negotiating instead of trying to intimidate each other, tensions have eased considerably.

But a chilling warning of Bible prophecy challenges our present peace and security:

> When they say, "Peace and safety!" then sudden destruction comes upon them, as labor pains upon a pregnant woman. And they shall not escape (1 Thessalonians 5:3).

Thank God, we don't have to be caught off guard:

> But you, brethren, are not in darkness, so that this Day should overtake you as a thief. . . . Therefore let us not sleep, as others do, but let us watch and be sober (1 Thessalonians 5:4-6).

These are sobering times. We must be alert.

In the 1890s, there was no thought of mass extermination from nuclear or chemical war. Now, besides those awful threats, we have another bomb bursting upon us: overpopulation, with three-and-a-half times as many people alive now as lived on this planet a century ago. Back then, we didn't have widespread famines with millions starving overseas. Now, even in this land of plenty, hungry people roam our streets, many of them addicted to alcohol and cocaine.

A century ago Americans cherished respect for authority. That was before Watergate. Today even parents are not respected as they once were. Television sitcoms poke fun at parental authority, especially dad. Without the moral absolutes of God's Law, society is decaying—all of this in tragic fulfillment of prophecy. The apostle Paul predicted:

> But know this, that in the last days perilous times will come: For men will be lovers of themselves, lovers of money, boasters, proud, blasphemers, disobedient to parents, unthankful, unholy, unloving, unforgiving, slanderers, without self-control, brutal, despisers of good (2 Timothy 3:1-3).

A century ago it was safe to walk the streets of our cities. People even left their doors unlocked. Now our cities have become war zones of gangs and drugs. Mass murderers terrorize entire metropolitan areas. It was back in the 1960s when our society began flirting with unrestrained freedom. "Doing your own thing," they called it, all in the name of peace and love. But the erosion of morality swept us into the gutter of pain and shame. We suffer the heartache of teenage pregnancy, alcoholism, and drug addiction, not to mention vandalism, violence, and sexually transmitted disease.

All this has resulted from rejecting God's standard of moral absolutes, His Ten Commandments. Look at the type of people the Bible predicted would populate our world in the end time:

> Traitors, headstrong, haughty, lovers of
> pleasure rather than lovers of God, having a
> form of godliness but denying its power
> (2 Timothy 3:4, 5).

The most disturbing thing about our current spiritual decay is that religious leaders have led the way into immoral pleasure seeking. A century ago Americans had spiritual leaders they felt they could trust. Evangelist Dwight L. Moody, by the time he retired in 1892, had won the respect of millions. In 1895 Billy Sunday took up the torch and began preaching to huge, attentive crowds. But now, for too many Americans, organized religion has become a joke—especially with the unthinkable scandals among religious broadcasters. Thank God for faithful ones like Billy Graham, who live above reproach. Other voices of faithfulness and integrity ring true as well. I'm thinking of James Dobson with his "Focus on the Family," and my good friend Lloyd Ogilvie. Many others too. One of the most important voices of our time is Chuck Colson, formerly of Watergate fame, who with his Prison Fellowship organization is accomplishing great good.

Although there has been a revival of religious interest in recent years, much of what passes for faith these days is nothing more than "give me what I want" selfishness. "Claim your miracle," they say. "Get what you want from God." But tell me, don't you think we should rather think of what God wants for our lives—after all, He created us!

You see my concern here. Another matter of deep distress is the environment. Americans in the 1890s never had to worry about acid rain or the greenhouse effect of the shrinking ozone layer. But now pollution has ravaged mother earth. Ecologists fear that irreversible damage may have been done to our world.

In March of 1989, a ruptured oil tanker spilled 11 million gallons of thick crude into Alaska's Prince William Sound and beyond. Cleanup workers onshore, being paid $16.73 an hour, scrubbed off the grime from potato-sized rocks, one by one. It was a futile and pitiful attempt to undo the irreversible damage suffered.

As we consider the way things have been going in our world, with all the pollution, the weaponry, the crime and immorality, positive thinking seems almost irrational. Can our world even last until the end of the decade? What happens when terrorist madmen get their restless fingers on the nuclear trigger?

But let's take courage, friend. Help is on the way. God has wonderful things in store for His committed people after Jesus comes:

> Nevertheless we, according to His promise, look for new heavens and a new earth in which righteousness dwells (2 Peter 3:13).

Thank God, our Lord Jesus Christ will cleanse this old planet of all its crime, all its pollution, all its selfishness, weaponry, and war. Peace on earth at last—what a day that will be!

A foretaste of this peace on earth happened, incredibly, on a battlefield during World War I. As reported in *Guideposts* magazine, it took place on Christmas Eve, 1914. In the rugged countryside of France, British and German troops had dug miles-long trenches, from which they blasted each other with machine guns and mortars.

Between the German and British trenches lay a

barren no man's land, a narrow strip of craters and shattered trees where anything that moved was shot. Whenever there was a lull in the firing, the shivering men on both sides could hear the noise of cooking going on in the enemy trenches.

Late on Christmas Eve, with freezing rain still falling and the temperature dropping, a British guard heard a new sound wafting across no man's land. In the enemy trenches a man was singing: "Stille Nacht, Heilige Nacht." It was a tune the British sentry recognized as "Silent Night, Holy Night." He began to hum along with the melody. Then a second British soldier crawled over and joined in. Soon others on both sides began blending their rough voices across the war-torn battlefield.

The Germans offered a second carol, "O Tannenbaum," and the British responded with "God Rest You Merry, Gentlemen." On and on through the night the singing continued. As dawn broke, signs appeared on both sides, in two languages, "Merry Christmas!"

Then, incredibly, one by one the soldiers laid down their guns and crawled beneath the barbed wire into no man's land, scores of British and German troops meeting together. The soldiers opened their wallets and showed off pictures of their families and exchanged gifts of candy.

This experience, surely one of history's most remarkable occurrences on any battlefield, has come to be known as the Soldier's Truce. Tragically, it was over all too soon. By mid-morning Christmas day, furious officers ordered their men back to the trenches. Soon the deadly bullets were whizzing back and forth again. Later that day a command came from British headquarters forbidding such contact: "We are here to fight, not to fraternize!"

Nevertheless, for a few hours the master of those soldiers was neither the kaiser or an earthly king, but heaven's Prince of Peace.

And thank God, the day is coming when that same Lord of glory will break through the clouds and put an end to war! An end to pollution, greed, and crime. The peace of God will reign unchallenged throughout this purified planet.

Where will you be on that day, my friend? Will you be shivering in the trenches of sin, or will you be rejoicing with God's committed people, saying, "Lo, this is our God, we have waited for Him, and He has come to save us!"

Chapter 2

Pornography's Fatal Attraction

Tuesday morning, January 24, 1989. As the golden sun rose over grassy fields outside Florida State Prison, a black veil dropped over the face of Theodore Robert Bundy. At 7:16 a.m., the 42-year-old serial murderer was pronounced dead in the electric chair.

In childhood, Ted Bundy was a respectful and respectable Boy Scout who attended Sunday School. What changed him into a murdering maniac? Bundy blamed an addiction to pornography for inflaming his deadly passion.

Across the road from Florida State Prison, news of Bundy's death sparked a celebration among the waiting crowd. They cheered. They lighted Roman candles. They even banged on frying pans proclaiming, "Tuesday is Fry-day."

We can understand their anger at Ted Bundy. If anyone deserved society's ultimate penalty, perhaps he did. Even so, thoughtful minds are distressed by the Mardi Gras atmosphere that prevailed outside the prison. The crowd even cheered when the white hearse drove past, bearing Bundy's body.

Relief, yes, that would be appropriate. Bundy had terrorized entire regions of the country with his awful crimes. He lured dozens of young women into trusting him, often by pretending to be injured or handicapped. Then he subjected them to gruesome torture before snuffing out their lives.

Colorado police captured Bundy, but he escaped to Florida, where he continued his murderous rampage. Finally corralled and brought to justice, Bundy played the part of his own lawyer at this trial, toying with the legal system. Sentenced at last to death row, he remained unsubdued, smugly disclaiming his guilt. When pressed by a reporter about one particularly hideous murder, he scoffed: "What's one less person on the face of the earth, anyway?"

Outrageous, incredible insensitivity! How could a good boy from a Christian home become perhaps the most feared and hated man in America?

Bundy himself answered that question in an interview with Dr. James C. Dobson, psychologist and broadcaster with Focus on the Family, a non-profit media organization dedicated to preservation of the family. The dramatic death row dialogue took place just hours before Bundy's execution. Look and listen now as Ted Bundy tells his own story:

DOBSON: For the record, you are guilty of killing many women and girls.
BUNDY: Yes. Yes. That's true.
DOBSON: Let's go back, then, to those roots. First of all, you, as I understand it, were raised in what you consider to have been a healthy home.
BUNDY: Absolutely.
DOBSON: You were not physically abused; you were not sexually abused; you were not emotionally abused.
BUNDY: No. No way. That's part of the tragedy of this whole situation, because I grew up in a wonderful

home with two dedicated and loving parents. I'm one of five brothers and sisters. [It was] a home where we as children were the focus of my parents' lives, where we regularly attended church. [I had] two Christian parents who did not drink; they did not smoke; there was no gambling; there was no physical abuse or fighting in the home. I'm not saying this was "Leave It to Beaver."

DOBSON: It wasn't a perfect home.

BUNDY: No, I don't know that such a home ever exists, but it was a fine, solid Christian home, and I hope no one will try to take the easy way out and blame or otherwise accuse my family of contributing to this because I know, and I'm trying to tell you as honestly as I know how, what happened. I think this is the message I want to get across. But as a young boy—and I mean a boy of twelve or thirteen certainly—I encountered, outside the home again, . . . in the local grocery store and the local drugstores the soft-core pornography, what people call "soft core." But as I think I explained to you last night, Dr. Dobson, in an anecdote, that as young boys do, we explored the back roads and sideways and byways of our neighborhood, and oftentimes people would dump the garbage and whatever they were cleaning out of the house. From time to time we'd come across pornographic books of a harder nature, more graphic you might say, [of] a more explicit nature than we would encounter, let's say, in your local grocery store. And this also included such things as detective magazines.

DOBSON: And those that involved violence, then.

BUNDY: Yes, and this is something I think I want to emphasize as the most damaging kinds of pornography, and again I'm talking from personal experience—hard, real, personal experience. The most damaging kinds of pornography are those that involve violence and sexual violence. Because the wedding of those two forces, as I know only too well, brings about behavior that is just too terrible to describe.

DOBSON: Now walk me through that. What was going on in your mind at that time?

BUNDY: OK, but before we go any further, I think it's important to me that people believe what I'm saying. I'm not blaming pornography; I'm not saying that it caused me to go out and do certain things. And I take full responsibility for whatever I've done. That's not the question here. The question and the issue is how this kind of literature contributed [to] and helped mold and shape the kinds of violent behavior.

DOBSON: It fueled your fantasies.

BUNDY: In the beginning it fuels this kind of thought process. Then at a certain time it's instrumental in what I would say crystallizing it, making it into something which is almost like a separate entity inside. At that point you're at the verge, or I was at the verge of acting out on these kinds of thoughts.

DOBSON: Now I really want to understand that. You had gone about as far as you could go in your own fantasy life with printed material, and then there was the urge to take that little step or big step over to a physical event.

BUNDY: Right. And it happened in stages, gradually. It doesn't necessarily—not to me at least—happen overnight. My experience with pornography that deals on a violent level with sexuality is that once you become addicted to it—and I look at this as a kind of addiction, like other kinds of addiction—I would keep looking for more potent, more explicit, more graphic kinds of materials. Like an addiction, you keep craving something harder, harder. Something which gives you a greater sense of excitement. Until you reach the point where the pornography only goes so far. You reach that jumping-off point where you begin to wonder if maybe actually doing it will give you that which is beyond just reading about it or looking at it.

DOBSON: How long did you stay at that point before you actually assaulted someone?

BUNDY: I would say a couple of years. What I was dealing with there were strong inhibitions against criminal behavior—violent behavior—that had been conditioned into me, bred into me, in my environment, in my neighborhood, in my church, in my school. Things which said no, this is wrong. I mean, even to think of this is wrong, but certainly to do it is wrong. And I'm on that edge, and these last . . . you might say, the last vestiges of restraint—the barriers to actually doing something—were being tested constantly and assailed through the kind of fantasy life that was fueled largely by pornography.

DOBSON: In the early days, you were nearly always about half-drunk when you did these things. Is that right?

BUNDY: Yes. Yes.

DOBSON: Was that always true?

BUNDY: I would say that was generally the case. Almost without exception.

DOBSON: All right, if I can understand it now, there's this battle going on within. There are the convictions that you've been taught. There's the right and wrong that you learned as a child. And then there is this unbridled passion fueled by your plunge into hard-core, violent pornography. And those things are at war with each other.

BUNDY: Yes.

DOBSON: And then with the alcohol diminishing the inhibitions, you let go.

BUNDY: Well, yes.

DOBSON: Ted, after you committed your first murder, what was the emotional effect on you? What happened in the days after that?

BUNDY: To wake up in the morning and realize what

I had done, with a clear mind and all my essential moral and ethical feelings intact at that moment, [I was] absolutely horrified that I was capable of doing something like that.

DOBSON: You really hadn't known that before?

BUNDY: There is just absolutely no way to describe—first the brutal urge to do that kind of thing, and then what happens. I want people to understand this, too, and I'm not saying this gratuitously, because it's important that people understand . . . that basically I was a normal person. I wasn't some guy hanging out at bars, or a bum. Or I wasn't a pervert in the sense that [you could] look at somebody and say, I know there's something wrong with him, and just tell. But I was essentially a normal person. I had good friends. I lived a normal life, except for this one small, but very potent, very destructive segment that I kept very secret, very close to myself, and didn't let anybody know about it.

And I think people need to recognize that those of us who have been so much influenced by violence in the media—in particular pornographic violence—are not some kinds of inherent monsters. We are your sons, and we are your husbands. And we grew up in regular families. And pornography can reach out and snatch a kid out of any house today. It snatched me out of my home twenty, thirty years ago, as diligent as my parents were, and they were diligent in protecting their children. And as good a Christian home as we had—and we had a wonderful Christian home—there is not protection against the kinds of influences that there are loose in a society that tolerates [pornography].

Listen. I'm no social scientist, and I haven't done a survey. I mean, I don't pretend that I know what John Q. Citizen thinks about this. But I've lived in prison for a long time now. And I've met a lot of men who were motivated to commit violence just like me. And without exception, every one of them was deeply involved in pornography—without question, without exception—deeply influenced and consumed by an addiction to pornography. There's no question about it. The FBI's own study on serial homicide shows that the most common interest among serial killers is pornography.

DOBSON: That's true.

BUNDY: And it's real. It's true. But I'll tell you, there are lots of other kids playing in the streets around this country today who are going to be dead tomorrow and the next day and the next day and next month, because other young people are reading the kinds of things and seeing the kinds of things that are available in the media today.*

What a heart-rending, eye-opening conversation! I'd like to thank Dr. Dobson and Focus on the Family for the permission to share portions of that copyrighted interview.

Some critics suggest that Bundy's testimony was just a desperate last-ditch attempt to save his life. That could not be true, though, since the interview had been in the planning stages for the previous six months. Other critics accused Dr. Dobson of interfering with Florida's criminal justice system by trying to delay Bundy's execution, or get it overturned. Again, such a charge is completely false. Dr. Dobson acknowledges that if any criminal deserved to die, Ted Bundy did. Focus on the Family only provided Bundy the opportunity he requested to warn the world about pornography's fatal attraction.

---

*Copyright© 1989 Focus on the Family; all rights reserved, international copyright secured.

Pornography has many defenders among those who find it personally distasteful. They defend its existence to protect their own constitutional right of free speech, wanting to avoid censorship at all costs. Actually, though, don't all of us believe in censorship to some degree? What responsible person would defend child pornography, the criminal exploitation of children? Obviously certain boundaries must be enforced—unlimited free expression cannot exist.

The key question here is, Where do we draw the line? Well, what did our founders have in mind when they guaranteed free speech in the First Amendment? Those who study history know that Jefferson, Madison, and Washington were guarding against religious and political repression. Do you think they would have risked their lives so that bloodthirsty audiences could be inspired by the *Texas Chainsaw Massacre?*

How long can a sane society tolerate this shocking, revolting abuse of women? Must we put up with an avalanche of violence and smut to protect the First Amendment?

Greedy pornographers keep reminding us about their First Amendment rights. But don't women and children have rights too? The right to walk our streets without fear of being attacked?

Some suggest, "If you don't like pornography, don't buy it; don't look at it; stay away from it." I'm afraid they miss the point. Others are buying, others are consuming pornography—criminals like Ted Bundy. And when those who are prone to violence view the violence in hard-core pornography, they seem to hear an evil voice whispering, "Go and do thou likewise."

Listen. If pornography triggers only a tenth of one percent of American men into committing criminal acts, nearly 10,000 rapists and murderers would be unleashed.

Evidently we can and we must oppose pornography because it threatens the public good. Not on the basis of religious preference, you understand, since faith cannot be legislated. Our goal is simply a safe society.

We heard in the Bundy interview that soft-core pornography, such as *Playboy* magazine, provides a gateway to hard-core, violent pornography. It also may contribute to the staggering divorce rate.

Think about it. So many men are abandoning their wives for younger women. Can we doubt that one reason for this is that pornography has spoiled their appreciation for what they already had at home?

This divorce epidemic burdens our already overworked court system. Worse yet, boys without a father around are more likely to become criminals. Pornography must shoulder some of the blame for America's fragmented families. Please ponder this final comment from Ted Bundy:

> I can only hope that those [whom] I have harmed and those [whom] I have caused so much grief—even if they don't believe my expression of sorrow and remorse—will believe what I'm saying now, that there is loose in their towns, in their communities, people like me today whose dangerous impulses are being fueled day in and day out by violence in the media in its various forms, particularly sexualized violence. And that scares me.

A sobering warning indeed, for all who have ears to hear.

Many have wondered whether Ted Bundy

repented of his awful crimes. Only God knows, of course, but indications are that he did finally repent and trust Jesus as his Saviour.

We hope so. But some seem to doubt that God could forgive Ted Bundy. Why? Isn't there power in the blood of our Lord Jesus Christ to forgive the most terrible sinner? Jesus promised: "The one who comes to Me I will by no means cast out" (John 6:37).

Come with me back to the mid-1970s, the days following Watergate. After Chuck Colson was released from prison, he didn't forget the men and women still behind bars. One day in 1981, with a team from his Prison Fellowship ministry, he was visiting the Indiana State Penitentiary. As Chuck recalls in his book *Loving God,* the group made their way through the maze of concrete cellblocks to the double set of barred doors leading to death row. The warden opened the individual cell doors, and one by one the condemned men timidly ventured out to mix with Colson and his volunteers.

Colson shared a brief message from the Bible; then all of them joined hands to sing "Amazing Grace." Following prayer, Colson's group bade goodbye to the prisoners and began filing out. They were crowding into a caged area between two massive gates when they noticed that one of their group was missing. Colson went back to get the man.

The volunteer, a short white man in his early fifties, was standing shoulder to shoulder with a young black man, reading together from a Bible. "I'm sorry. We have to leave," Colson urged, glancing at his watch.

After all, the schedule was tight. A plane waited outside to whisk Colson to a meeting with the governor.

The volunteer looked up. "Give us just a minute, please. This is important," he said softly. Then he added, "You see, I'm Judge Clement, the one who sentenced James Brewer here to die. But now he's my brother, and we want a minute to pray together."

Colson recalled, "I stood frozen in the cell doorway. It didn't matter who I kept waiting. Before me were two men: one was powerless, the other powerful; one was black, the other white—and one had sentenced the other to death. Anywhere other than the kingdom of God, that inmate might have killed the judge with his bare hands—or wanted to anyway. Now they were one in Christ, their faces reflecting an indescribable expression of love as they prayed together."

On the way out of the prison, Judge Clement told Colson that every day for four years since he had sentenced Brewer to death, he had been praying for his salvation. Thank God, those prayers had been answered.

Yes, James Brewer was a saved man there on death row. Both judge and condemned prisoner stood clean before the Lord, equal in God's sight— equally lost outside of Christ; equally saved in Christ. You see, heaven comes to us not because we are worthy, but because we have entrusted our lives to the Lord Jesus Christ, who died for our sins on Calvary's cross.

My friend, the amazing grace of God that saved Judge Clement and James Brewer is your only hope, and mine as well. What's more, the same transforming grace that united the hearts of those courtroom foes can renew our relationships too. Whatever master passion may enslave the soul, there is power in the Lord Jesus Christ to overcome. I urge you to give your life to Him just now.

Chapter 3

The Truth About AIDS

They called it the tunnel of love—a hallway with an arched ceiling leading past doorways wreathed in marijuana smoke. From the dimly-lighted rooms along the tunnel came the sounds of men engaged in homosexual acts.

Were health officials justified in closing down this Los Angeles area gay bathhouse? What should society do to protect itself against AIDS?

Every Saturday night, yuppie-type young men congregated at the gay bathhouse. They traded their trousers for towels and chose partners for the evening. By eight o'clock a No Vacancy sign went up, informing disappointed latecomers that all fifty rooms were occupied.

Citizen's groups condemned the bathhouse as a moral blight on its suburban neighborhood. Then a local newspaper exposed the place as a hotbed for breeding the deadly disease AIDS. Finally the county health inspector closed the facility.

They may have sealed off the so-called tunnel of love, but they opened up a controversy about what to do with homosexual promiscuity and the risk of AIDS. All around our nation, no issue generates more controversy than what rights homosexuals have in the light of the AIDS epidemic.

Much remains unknown about this deadly disease, making it difficult to sift rumor from fact. Several truths about AIDS are certain, though.

First of all, while AIDS is a threat to all groups, it is especially dangerous for two groups: IV drug users and homosexuals, specifically homosexual men. You understand I'm not a medical researcher, so there is nothing I can contribute to the ongoing analysis of the disease itself. The best course for anyone is to avoid high risk behavior. Education itself is not enough—people need to take responsibility.

We hear much talk about safe sex. True, certain precautions can greatly reduce the risk of getting AIDS, but the only sure safeguard is old-fashioned biblical morality. The truth about AIDS is this: there is no such thing as safe sin. In addition to terrible physical risk, there are definite spiritual consequences of living out of harmony with God's Law. Even innocent children and spouses suffer the deadly results of others' homosexual immorality.

Lest anyone doubt what the Bible says about the practice of homosexuality, it would be well to notice this passage from the book of Romans:

> Because of this, God gave them over to shameful lusts. Even their women exchanged natural relations for unnatural ones. In the same way the men also abandoned natural relations with women and were inflamed with lust for one another. Men committed indecent acts with other men, and received in themselves the due penalty for their perversion (Romans 1:26, 27, NIV).

There can be little question where the Bible

stands on homosexual behavior. We must reap what we sow. Sooner or later, immorality of any kind yields a harvest of pain and loss. But let's remember this: Homosexuals need our help and understanding, not condemnation. We must not judge fellow sinners, but rather offer them spiritual guidance and human compassion.

You know, sooner or later this discussion about homosexuality involves the personal lives of people. People like Jim. Back in the sixties, he had enrolled in a Christian college, hoping that the wholesome environment there would help him suppress his homosexual tendencies and harmonize his life with God's commandments. Jim won many friends among his fellow students, none of whom suspected the secret fire raging in his flesh. Only one person understood—Jim's roommate, who eventually became his sexual partner.

Since Jim was a courteous and caring sort of guy, several nice girls wanted to date him. He managed to avoid them, though, joking that he ought to study more than socialize.

Meanwhile, Jim slipped deeper and deeper into homosexuality, trying to rationalize his behavior as acceptable to God. In his senior year he committed himself to the gay lifestyle. By the way, you understand, Jim's name and some of his circumstances are changed here to protect his privacy.

One day at church he responded to an altar call and pledged to read his Bible every day. That's how he came across the text we read in Romans 1, which convinced him that homosexuality was indeed a sin.

Jim repented. He found a new roommate and forced himself to associate with girls. All this with the prayer that God would give him normal sexual desires.

Jim formed a brother-sister relationship with Linda, a sophomore nursing major. Their friendship flourished into romance. After Jim's graduation they got married.

It proved to be a tragedy. Although Jim was kind to Linda and their baby, the marriage floundered. Before long, Linda discovered Jim's dark secret—he had an affair going with his former roommate.

Shocked by Jim's homosexuality, she divorced him. Well, the bottom fell out of Jim's life. He deserved it, certainly, since he had betrayed Linda's love and destroyed their home. Just the same, it was sad. All Jim's friends forsook him. Even his church shunned him. So he stopped attending services and joined the gay community.

What a shame! Back in his teenage years, Jim hadn't intended to become homosexual. He just found himself attracted to boys rather than girls. For twenty agonizing years he fought with the flesh. Finally, after the divorce, he abandoned himself to unbridled homosexuality.

Jim campaigned for gay rights, craving society's approval of his perversion. But really, Jim himself couldn't approve of it—his own conscience frowned upon him. He even secretly hated himself.

Jim feared that sooner or later his sexual adventures would infect him with the dread disease AIDS, yet he couldn't make himself stop to save his life. Not even for the sake of his eternal life. Sin had him hopelessly enslaved.

Jim's former friends at church condemned him as insincere and lacking in spiritual commitment. They didn't notice the quiet sadness in his eyes, the deep disappointment and consternation. But God knew Jim was more a victim than a villain.

Jim would have been shocked to learn that many of the saints who raised their eyebrows at him failed miserably in dealing with their own temptations. In the sight of God, Jim's homosexuality was no worse than the sinful habits of other church members. In fact, Jesus reserved His most stern warnings for the self-righteous and spiritually proud, the very ones who condemned the poor slaves of immorality.

We all suffer from sinfulness, whatever our level of Christian growth. All of us have spiritual AIDS, you might say. AIDS, you probably know, stands for Acquired Immune Deficiency Syndrome—a condition that prevents the body from resisting disease. Well, our sinful nature has crippled our spiritual immune system. We can't resist sin by ourselves. It's a condition we acquired, or inherited, at birth.

Even the apostle Paul suffered a spiritual immune deficiency. Here's how he described the problem: "What I do is not the good I want to do; no, the evil I do not want to do—this I keep on doing" (Romans 7:19, NIV).

Paul couldn't fend off sin, much as he tried to live a pure life:

> For in my inner being I delight in God's law; but I see another law at work in the members of my body, waging war against the law of my mind and making me a prisoner of the law of sin at work within my members. What a wretched man I am! Who will rescue me from this body of death? (Romans 7:22-24, NIV).

A body of death—spiritual AIDS. Remember, Paul's heart was in the right place. In this whole chapter of Romans 7 you see nothing but wholehearted yearning after goodness, total dedication to pleasing God. But Paul discovered, to his dismay, that he was allergic to religion.

Perhaps you suffer an allergy to something you like. Likewise, Paul delighted in God's law, but his flesh was allergic to it: "We know that the law is spiritual; but I am unspiritual, sold as a slave to sin" (Romans 7:14, NIV).

So despite his enthusiasm and unreserved commitment, Paul failed miserably. Just like Jim. Like us too? But must we remain the helpless slaves of sin? Is there no power in the gospel to change our lives? It's nice to know God forgives us when we sin—but don't we also want His power to conquer the countless temptations that come our way every day?

The apostle Paul at last discovered the secret of personal power. We find it in Romans 6:14: "Sin shall not be your master, because you are not under law, but under grace" (NIV).

Good news here. Slavery to sin ends when we learn to live "not under law but under grace." Just what does this mean? Let's go back to Jim and find out.

When he first got married, he determined to measure up to the law "Thou shalt not commit adultery." He struggled valiantly to obey God's commandments. But the more he tried to suppress his unlawful homosexual tendencies, the stronger they became.

Of course, nothing was wrong with the law itself. But something happened when the law pointed out Paul's guilt:

> Sin, taking opportunity by the commandment, produced in me all manner of evil desire. For apart from the law sin was dead (Romans 7:8).

Amazing, isn't it? Our sinful nature takes advantage of the commandment "Do not covet," to produce the very behavior forbidden. And this despite our earnest commitment to obey God's holy law.

Now we can understand why Jim succumbed spiritually. The law condemned his homosexual cravings, so naturally he felt guilty. Despondent, he figured, "What's the use anyway?" Utterly depressed, he plunged back over the cliff into the depths of immorality.

Jim did feel terrible about breaking God's commandments and betraying his marriage vows, but all the guilt in the world didn't help him stop sinning. Condemnation only compounded the sin problem.

Jim actually felt relieved when Linda finally found him out. He had been dropping hints, leaving clues about what he was doing, hoping to be caught so he could stop living a lie.

After Linda divorced Jim, he divorced himself from religion. Living under the law had been such a burden, such a source of guilt. With sincere regrets to God and His commandments, Jim resumed his gay lifestyle.

And why did it happen? The holy law of God condemns our guilt and leaves us discouraged, driving us deeper and deeper into sin. And the deeper we fall into sin, the more we feel condemned. It's a vicious cycle. How nice it would be to flee from condemnation into the comforting arms of Jesus. And such an escape is possible! We can be fully and freely forgiven in the Lord Jesus Christ.

Sinners can find acceptance with God because our Saviour's life and death fulfilled the law's requirements on our behalf. This is the good news of the gospel. But does saving grace release us from spiritual responsibility? Are we free now to live as we please?

Not at all. Notice what the Bible says: "You . . . died to the law through the body of Christ . . . that we might bear fruit to God" (Romans 7:4).

This is victory over sin, contrasting with the "fruit for death" we bore in the old life.

What a difference here from the old life of legalism! The new atmosphere of acceptance and assurance sparks a spiritual growth spurt. Sin loses its dominion, and we bear the fruit of Christian love—we actually find ourselves honoring those same commandments that we felt were so oppressive.

Of course, we still fall short of God's glorious ideal, but no sincere believer need yield to despair:

> There is therefore now no condemnation to those who are in Christ Jesus (Romans 8:1).

Now, let's get back to Jim—his story has a happy ending. He finally came to realize that God really loved him, despite his failure and confusion. He learned he didn't have to qualify himself for heaven by competing with Christ's perfect character. Gladly he found refuge in the Saviour's mercy, crying, "Jesus, Son of David, have mercy on me." And thanks to Calvary, God could now say, "This is Jim, My beloved son, in whom I am well pleased."

Well, the Lord's grace has worked miracles in Jim's life. With guilt gone, sin's vicious cycle has ended. Jim, confident of God's forgiveness, doesn't get discouraged as easily as before. The joy of the Lord strengthens him to conquer whatever temptations come his way.

Jim visits a licensed Christian counselor for help in his recovery. He wondered why he had been attracted to men all these years—some researchers insist that homosexuality is genetically predetermined; others vigorously disagree. Either way, Jim's counselor told him, it doesn't really matter. everyone enters this world with a fallen nature, suffering sinful predispositions of one kind or another.

Some may be especially susceptible to alcoholism. Others to obesity. Still others to violence and abuse. Women appear more prone to become depressed. Men seem to struggle more with physical lust.

Jim used to envy heterosexual men because marriage provides a legitimate outlet for their natural sex drive. His counselor explained that even married men can't indulge their fantasies. You see, God expects all of us to refrain from immorality; otherwise, society would collapse in chaos. So nobody can excuse indulging in sin, no matter what the individual predisposition may be. Living under grace provides power to overcome. Thank God, He also offers mercy when we fail to fulfill our potential.

Jim now believes he became a homosexual because he lacked a fulfilling relationship with his father. His sexual adventurism was an unconscious attempt to find the paternal love he never knew. One expert asserts: "No child becomes homosexual if there has been a warm, emotional relationship with the father."

Other factors also contributed to Jim's homosexuality. As a boy he never had a male role model, and because of this he never managed to develop his own masculine identity. He felt less competent than his peers in relating to girls, and thus he shied away from intimacy with the opposite sex. Feeling inadequate as a man, he formed "safe" relationships where he didn't have to play the male role. So Jim's low self-esteem also influenced homosexual behavior.

Jim had been borrowing masculinity from other men through his perverted relationships. But he's slowly learning to assert himself as a man in his own right, as much a man as anyone else. And now that Jim has a fulfilling relationship with his Father in heaven, he doesn't yearn so much for the support of earthly men.

I wish I could tell you Jim doesn't have homosexual cravings now. Unfortunately, some of that remains. If it weren't for God's keeping power, Jim would certainly drift back into homosexual practice.

As long as we remain on this earth our sinful flesh will harass us with temptation:

> The flesh lusts against the Spirit, and the Spirit against the flesh; and these are contrary to one another, so that you do not do the things that you wish (Galatians 5:17).

All Christians experience this battle between two opposing forces—the old nature of the flesh and the new nature of the Spirit. And so Jim finds himself haunted by habits he formed in years past. These attractions and feelings annoy Jim, but they don't amount to sin—as long as he refuses to yield to them. Jim isn't a homosexual anymore because he no longer practices that lifestyle.

And now, my friend reading these pages, what about you? You may be struggling with homosexuality or with adultery or some other private sin. Maybe you're about to give up. Please

don't. Remember that God loves you. He will forgive you completely and immediately, if you will
entrust your life to Him in the name of Jesus
Christ.

Chapter 4

Addiction: Disease or Sin?

A war is raging in Washington, bigger than any battle on Capitol Hill. It's happening on the streets of our nation's capital. People are murdering each other, all for the sake of a vial of crack, a crystallized derivative of cocaine.

Are cocaine addicts the victims of a disease? And what about addiction to alcohol and tobacco—is that a disease, or dare we call it sin? Either way, help is in store if you need it. And America needs a lot of help with its addictions. Pushers and addicts prowl the streets of our nation's cities. Needing money to sustain their habits, prostitutes and robbers haunt the alleyways. People even commit murder for the sake of a vial of crack.

The nation's southern border is a sieve for drug traffic. Our frustrated police have been fighting a losing battle—for every drug lord they do manage to catch, two seem to take his place. And most disturbing of all, Americans have an insatiable demand for that chemical high.

Small wonder the drug issue emerged during the 1988 presidential campaign as America's number one problem. President Bush on his inauguration day reemphasized his pledge to fight drug abuse. I was sitting on the platform behind our newly sworn-in leader as he spoke his heartfelt words concerning drug addiction: "This scourge must end!"

The scourge of drug addiction is particularly vicious in the President's back yard. As evidence for this, in 1988 the city of Washington had the highest homicide rate in the nation. When the killing skyrocketed further during the first quarter of 1989, something drastic had to be done, and quickly. President Bush appointed William Bennett as the new Director of the White House Office of National Drug Control Policy, the federal drug czar. With a challenge even bigger than his title, Bennett launched an unprecedented assault on Washington's drug problem. It was an $80-million project to crack down on dealers and their cohorts in crime.

Helpless parents realize that law enforcement is not enough to save their children from drug addiction. They wonder what to tell their teenagers—especially when the younger generation points to the inconsistency of many adults. They say, "You call me an addict, but what about your drinking? Isn't alcohol a drug too? And what about your Marlboros with their nicotine?"

They have a point, we have to admit. Too many adults set a fatal example by harboring their own addictions. More than a thousand smokers a day are killed by their habit. And who can compute the cost of alcoholism in broken homes, broken bones, and broken promises?

Well, enough talk about the problem now. Let's look for solutions. The real battle must be won in the minds and hearts of consumers. Unless the demand for drugs dries up, suppliers will always find a way to smuggle in their dope.

So the demand for drugs, the addiction itself, must be confronted. This raises the question, Are we discussing a disease or a sin? The answer is important. You see, some suggest that addiction is a predetermined fate, something programmed from birth in one's genes. If that's true, how can you blame an addict for fulfilling his fate? But, on the other hand, if addiction is behavior that can be avoided, a sin to be shunned, there is no excuse for cocaine addiction or the tobacco habit or drunkenness.

Page one of our local paper carried the sad account of a drunken driver who killed three teenagers on Highway 101. They were walking along the side of the road, seeking help for their broken-down car, when her car struck them. Her blood alcohol level was twice the California legal limit of intoxication. Tragically, just the night before that same driver had been pulled over for drunken driving—and then released. Authorities are contemplating murder charges.

Well, if this driver is a helpless victim of a disease she could not control, then society ought not hold her responsible for the deaths of those teenagers. But if she had any kind of choice about getting drunk again the night she killed those kids, would she not bear responsibility?

Not long ago the Veterans Administration stirred up quite a controversy by challenging the belief that alcoholism is a disease. Actually, it wasn't until the sixties that this disease notion became popular. And many Christian psychologists and pastors, almost by default, accepted the conclusions of secular researchers. Now, however, some experts recognize that alcoholism is a problem of behavior rather than merely one of disease.

Herbert Fingarette is a consultant on alcoholism and addiction to the World Health Organization and a researcher at the Stanford Center for Advanced Studies and Behavioral Sciences. He recently wrote the book *Heavy Drinking: The Myth of Alcoholism As a Disease.* In it he suggested that thinking of addiction as a disease ignores human responsibility and "denies the spiritual dimension" of alcohol dependency.

Fingarette reminded us that no scientific evidence exists to indicate that alcoholics are unable to do something about their habit. It's a drinker's mind-set that determines alcohol consumption. These days, he added, "No leading authorities accept the classic disease concept" for alcoholism.

Suppose some people do suffer a genetic weakness for alcoholism. All of us suffer from compulsions and predispositions to sin in one way or another. And whenever we indulge these weaknesses, we must face the consequences. Alcoholics—and anyone else with an addiction—must also bear responsibility for their behavior. They are not helpless victims, in the same way the people they hurt are victimized.

Consider this. It might seem loving and compassionate to tell addicted friends that their problem is not their fault, that they are victims of a disease beyond their control. But think about it—what they are really hearing from us is that they are hopeless. That's not good news for them. And it's not true. Addicts can get up and get help. And until they do take responsibility for their addiction, they will never behave responsibly.

So let's encourage people that they can change. When we unite our will with God's strength, we can do all things through Christ. His love brings us power. More about this later.

You've seen the television ads urging addicts to get help for their problem. Obviously addictive behavior is avoidable, not like diseases for which you have no choice about getting help.

So alcoholism is a "behavior disorder," not just a "disease." And really, "behavior disorder" is just another way to say "sin."

What does the Bible say about addiction? Well, God's Word does not flatter human nature. It's quite frank about the sin problem all of us suffer: "The heart is deceitful above all things, and desperately wicked" (Jeremiah 17:9).

Now, this sin problem is considered a type of sickness. We read here: "The whole head is sick, and the whole heart faints" (Isaiah 1:5).

Evidently addiction can be considered a disease in the sense that all sin is a disease—but it's not a disease like the measles, over which we have no control. Since human responsibility is involved in addiction, we would expect the Bible to have some earnest warnings about such destructive behavior. And it does. In the New Testament the apostle Paul lists a number of sins, and notice what's included along with such things as adultery and hatred:

> Envy, murders, drunkenness, revelries, and the like; of which I tell you beforehand, just as I also told you in time past, that those who practice such things will not inherit the kingdom of God (Galatians 5:21).

Now that's a strong statement from the Word of God. Drunkenness is listed with a number of sinful practices that would disqualify us from heaven. Please understand, the Lord doesn't count us guilty when we have repented of our sins and honestly come to Him for help, even when we struggle and fail. What robs us of eternal life is a stubborn refusal to confront our sins and exchange them for what Jesus has to offer.

Remember the story Christ told about the prodigal son? That young man abandoned his father and left home for a far-off land, where he wasted himself away with wild living. Finally, the Bible says, he "came to himself." In other words, he confronted his behavior. Then he made the big decision and announced to himself: "I will arise and go to my father, and will say to him, 'Father, I have sinned against heaven and before you' " (Luke 15:18).

No more fooling around here. No more excuses. The prodigal took full responsibility for his drunken carousing and called it a sin: "I have sinned," he said. Then he did something about it— he took action and went home. You know the story. The father ran to welcome his repentant son, forgiving him fully and freely with the pronouncement: "This my son was dead and is alive again; he was lost and is found" (Luke 15:24).

Notice that the son had been lost, spiritually dead. Not just sick, but dead lost. Thank the Lord, though, now that the boy had confronted his addictive behavior and come home to father, he was alive and safe.

Alcoholics aren't lost because they drink, but only because they reject Jesus Christ as their refuge and find their solace in the bottle. Drug addicts aren't lost because of their cravings; it's just that they give themselves over to counterfeit fulfillment rather than to what Jesus offers.

Let's probe a little deeper here into the nature of sin, how yielding to addiction is a sin. Notice Romans 13:13, 14:

> Let us walk properly, as in the day, not in
> revelry and drunkenness, not in licentiousness
> and lewdness, not in strife and envy. But put
> on the Lord Jesus Christ, and make no pro-
> vision for the flesh, to fulfill its lusts.

All immorality, drunkenness included, is a poor substitute for having Jesus in our lives. When we are lonely, He wants us to find companionship in Him, not in sin. When we suffer stress, He invites us to come to Him and rest. When we are happy, He would be delighted for us to share our joy with Him.

For all the reasons people drink or take drugs—whether those drugs be cocaine or tobacco or whatever—Jesus wants us to depend upon Him instead. That's why the text we read tells us to "put on the Lord Jesus Christ." To have such a relationship, the Bible says, we must avoid making provision for the flesh to fulfill its lusts.

So just say No to sin—and say Yes to Jesus!

Now, let's make all this practical. If your struggle is with alcohol, clean out those six-packs from your refrigerator. Get rid of them. If cocaine is your problem, flush it down the drain. Do you smoke? Well, throw away those cigarettes.

Talk with your pastor. You may need professional counseling—but find someone who will hold you accountable for your habit. Don't trust those who think they know more than the Lord does about confronting and confessing our sin.

Above all, my friend, put Jesus first in your life! Remember, addictions are an expression of emptiness without Christ. We can find our fulfillment in Him and what He offers, rather than fooling around with the devil's counterfeits.

We have a very special reason to treat our bodies responsibly. The Lord Jesus sacrificed His life so that we might belong to Him:

> Do you not know that your body is a temple of the Holy Spirit, who is in you, whom you have received from God? You are not your own; you were bought at a price. Therefore honor God with your body (1 Corinthians 6:19, 20, NIV).

Think of it—the living, loving God takes up residence within our bodies and our minds! Naturally, such privilege is not without its responsibilities. If God makes our human body His temple, the least we can do is take care of it. Thoughtful Christians are recognizing this now.

Seventh-day Adventists, for more than a century, have understood that good religion takes an interest in good health. And so they lay aside tobacco and liquor and emphasize the advantages of exercise, fresh air, sunshine, and a balanced diet.

Does healthful living pay? It certainly does. The Adventist lifestyle—with its appetizing natural-food diet and its abstinence from alcohol and tobacco— helps them live six to seven years longer than the general population, according to research, with only half the cancer and heart disease.

Along with most conservative Christians, Seventh-day Adventists teach total abstinence from alcohol. How can it be otherwise, when we find in God's Word such instruction as 1 Corinthians 10:31? "Whether you eat or drink, or whatever you do, do all to the glory of God."

What is there about even one glass of wine that would glorify God? Do you think alcohol helps us become better parents and spouses? Does it make us more responsible citizens? Better workers? More faithful Christians?

No, friend, I can't think of anything about alcohol that glorifies God. Can you? Some say that an occasional glass of wine has medicinal benefit—but doctors these days suggest alternatives that don't have the loaded-gun potential of wine.

Evidently our only security from alcoholism is total abstinence. Addiction sneaks up unawares, ensnaring even cautious and responsible social drinkers. In a time of personal crisis, they find themselves depending more and more upon a drink, and afterward they often have trouble cutting down again. They're hooked.

And the cost in addiction is staggering, these days especially. Back in Bible times if a person got drunk he might have fallen off his donkey. These days, intoxication causes fatal accidents. And when you consider the rising divorce rate and the many temptations around to tarnish our integrity, how important it is in these last days to heed Scripture's warning about being sober and prayerful.

The Bible offers us a wonderful substitute for alcohol: "Do not get drunk on wine, which leads to debauchery. Instead, be filled with the Spirit" (Ephesians 5:18).

Just how are we filled with the Spirit? By entrusting our lives to Jesus day by day, yielding ourselves to God's guidance through His Word. Remember, to conquer alcohol, cocaine, tobacco, or anything else, it's not enough to "Just say no." That's important, but it's not enough. We must also say Yes to Jesus, entrusting our lives to Him. Then God's Spirit can empower us to honor Him with our bodies—His temple.

Let me tell you about Tom Benefiel. Once upon a

time he was a drug addict in Long Beach, California, living the wild life with his girlfriend. Then, without Tom's knowing about it, she started watching our "It Is Written" telecast, becoming a regular viewer. Soon she began having second thoughts about the way she was living with Tom. When I invited our telecast audience to attend a series of community meetings I was conducting, she attended. Somehow she managed to drag Tom along with her.

So there they were on the front row, Tom with his long hair and colorful beads. He wore a bright smile—but not because he was particularly happy to be at church. He was high on drugs, you see, and Tom always wore a big smile when he was high.

I saw him there smiling at me, so of course I smiled back. I didn't know why he was smiling; I just thought he was a happy hippie. But that night the good Lord opened the message of His love to Tom's drug-clouded mind.

Night after night he returned, always on the front row. The Holy Spirit worked repentance in his heart and won Him to Christ. A crucial point in Tom's conversion was when he decided to confront his drug problem and call that addiction a sin. Let me tell you, the day he was baptized was a glorious experience.

Now the question came, What should Tom do with his life? His twenty-seven-year-old body and mind had been ravaged by drugs. Gainful employment seemed impossible. Then the local pastor came up with a shocking suggestion—why not consider becoming a minister?

A minister, of all things? Tom prayed about the idea and recognized God's leading. A series of dramatic miracles opened the way for him to attend Loma Linda University, where Tom earned top grades.

The Lord healed Tom's drug-scarred mind. Upon his graduation, the Seventh-day Adventist Church hired him to work in a student witnessing program in Oxnard, California. That's where he met his sweet wife, Annie. Today they are a dynamic pastoral team, dear friends of mine, winning souls for the Lord Jesus Christ.

The Lord transformed Tom's life, bringing him the peace and power of Jesus Christ. And you know, He can do the same for you.

Chapter 5

The New Age Conspiracy

Powerful yet subtle, a new religious movement is gaining ground in America. It's called the New Age, and it's making astonishing inroads into unsuspecting Christianity.

Rumors are that New Age leaders have formed a conspiracy to take control of the world. Can that possibly be?

All around us, evidence abounds of the New Age religion. Drive down the highway, and you see those quartz crystals dangling from mirrors inside cars going by. Visit the mall, and you notice store racks stuffed with New Age paperbacks. Watch a TV talk show, and there's actress Shirley MacLaine, bubbling over with enthusiasm about the New Age.

What's going on? What is this New Age, anyway?

The New Age movement is a melting pot of pagan Eastern religion stirred up with occult spiritism and flavored with a pinch of Christianity—just enough to make New Age concepts tasteful to Western society.

The movement dates back to the 1960s—and the roots of its teachings go far beyond that—but it

55

wasn't until the eighties that the New Age had its burst of popularity. Now in the nineties it's becoming more aggressive than ever. Is there some sort of global conspiracy involved?

To find out, let's consult a book some New Agers treat as their Bible: *The Aquarian Conspiracy*, by Marilyn Ferguson. She speaks of the New Age movement as a "leaderless but powerful network" "working to bring about radical change in the United States."

So there is a network of New Agers working to revolutionize our society, but Ferguson claims they have no centralized leadership. This is true, so far as I can tell. I found no evidence of a human authority structure—nothing like a political party or religious organization.

However, Christian researcher and editor Kenneth Wade has an interesting suggestion about a conspiracy in his book *Secrets of the New Age* (p. 101):

> While it [the New Age movement] may not be a close-knit organization on the human level, in my reading I have turned up strong evidence that there is organization at the superhuman level that is working to knit together the network of people who are listening to the various spirits that proclaim the imminence of the New Age.

Is there a supernatural conspiracy here? Do spirit forces really control the worldwide New Age movement? There is no question that spirit beings are involved, constantly communicating New Age messages through meditation and channeling. Channelers, you may know, are humans who convey the spirit messages, often while in a trancelike state.

Now the important question: Who are these spirits? Are they angels from God or demons from the devil? Although many New Age spirits name themselves after Bible characters, their messages betray another source. They contradict Bible truth, as we will see. And this business of channeling resembles how the devil spoke to Eve in the Garden of Eden, when he communicated his deceptions through the serpent in order to plunge this world into ruin. The enemy's goal is the same today.

So here we have the real conspiracy: Satan and his fallen angels, using New Age meditation and channeling, intend to deceive the whole world—including you and me.

You may remember a song popular in the late sixties that proclaimed the dawning of the Age of Aquarius. This "Aquarian Age" is the New Age goal of a post-Christian era here on earth. How do New Agers think it will happen? The author of *The Aquarian Conspiracy* explains: "We have it within our power to make peace within our torn selves and with each other, to heal our homeland, the whole earth."

So New Age disciples imagine they can save the earth from war, crime, pollution, and every other threat. That's why they got together a couple of years ago for their Harmonic Convergence. One August weekend in 1987, New Age believers from around the world congregated in thirty-six spots they consider sacred. They met in places like the Grand Canyon, California's Mt. Shasta, the Pyramids of Egyp,t and Mt. Fuji in Japan.

You may have wondered what they were doing, holding hands in a circle and making that peculiar humming sound. Did you know they weren't really humming? They were voicing the Hindu word *Om.*

That tiny word *O-m* from the Hindu scriptures is supposed to have tremendous power, able to generate enough cosmic force to create a whole New Age of peace and love.

There was a reason New Agers choose that particular weekend of August 16. It was supposed to be the first time in 23,412 years that the heavens had positioned themselves to radiate ultimate cosmic power. Emile Canning, group leader on Shasta, implored, "144,000 sun dancers filled with the sun will bring on the New Age." World peace and relief from catastrophe would result. So they believed.

Well, they got their sun dancers that Sunday—more than the required 144,000—but hopes for a New Age failed them. That very night Northwest Flight 255 crashed in Detroit, the second-worst single air disaster in United States history up to that time. Hardly what the New Agers expected from their weekend of sun dancing.

Channeling was a big event at the Harmonic Convergence. Famous departed personalities supposedly disclosed their harmonic wishes through psychic mediums. In a meadow beneath Mt. Shasta's fir-covered slopes, 200 pilgrims from Los Angeles paid $35 each to listen reverently as John the Apostle (from Bible times, supposedly) spoke to them through channeler Jerry Bowman. So they imagined.

Well, it won't cost us $35 to know what the real apostle John said about the New Age. In the New Testament he pointed us toward the second coming of Jesus as our hope for the future—not the magical transformation of the earth here and now.

Another conflict between New Age teachings and the Christian faith involves reincarnation, the belief that human souls are recycled in this world from one life to the next. But, according to the Bible, we only live once in this world before Jesus comes: "It is appointed for men to die once, but after this the judgment" (Hebrews 9:27).

So we die once before we are judged. New Age reincarnation actually has its roots in Hindu and Buddhist belief, modified for the sake of Americans who want to feel good about themselves.

By the way, why do people who believe in reincarnation always seem to think they were someone important in ages past, maybe a royal knight of King Arthur's court? You seldom hear anyone testifying, "In my former life I shoveled manure!"

New Age author Corrine McLaughlin, writing for the publication *New Realities,* recognized the problem: "A further explanation for the popularity of channels now," she pointed out, "is that they tell people all the things their egos always wanted to hear: 'You can have anything you want; you deserve it; you're perfect just as you are, so you don't have to try harder to be a better person, etc.' "

Tell me. Do you want to be flattered by falsehood, or do you want to know the truth about yourself? McLaughlin herself said it best: "The only really sure way to avoid getting false information or being deceived or controlled by a psychic or channel—don't consult one in the first place!"

Now, there isn't much in New Age publications that I can agree with, but I'll say Amen to that!

Exhibit A of the enchanting deceptions involved in reincarnation is what happened to Shirley MacLaine. She first consulted a channeler trying to cope with a personal crisis. Determined to be objective, she was somewhat skeptical about this whole New Age business. But during the trance, suddenly the spirit entity being channeled revealed the secret affair MacLaine was having with a man named Gerry. What's more, he even quoted the very words the couple had spoken privately.

MacLaine was stunned. Compelled at the revelation, she put her faith in channeled entities. Her belief strengthened when another channeled spirit explained why she and Gerry felt such an attraction for each other. Why, they had been married in a previous life, so naturally they belonged together!

They belonged together—just what a nagging conscience would want to hear. MacLaine was hooked. She became an enthusiastic disciple of the New Age and is now one of the movement's foremost apostles.

America's current explosion of interest in channeling stems from a television miniseries based on MacLaine's New Age adventures. B. Dalton bookstores reported that sales of occult titles nearly doubled during the week in 1987 when MacLaine's miniseries first aired.

Tragically, even Christians are getting caught up in the excitement of a New Age. They don't realize the absolute conflict between what New Agers believe and what the Bible teaches. Ken Wade sums up the differences in his book:

> [The New Age] is a shift from . . . the Christian concept of a personal, caring God to the belief that human beings are their own god. It is a shift from belief in death, judgment, and resurrection to belief in reincarnation; from belief in heaven and hell to belief that we create our own heaven or hell right here on earth; from belief in the grace of God for sinners to belief that every individual must pay for his or her wrongs in repeated lives of suffering; from belief that there is a God in control of our destiny to belief that we must, through planned

evolution, improve our own lot" (pp. 31, 32).

Important information, wouldn't you say? Let's probe deeper into the vast difference between New Age teachings and Christianity. New Ager John Randolph Price made an astounding prediction in *The Superbeings:* "When man realizes his god identity, a race of gods will rule the universe."

Imagine the blasphemy—the human race being a race of gods! Is this not but an echo of the devil's first great lie channeled through the serpent? "The serpent said to the woman, 'You will not surely die. . . . You will be like God' " (Genesis 3:4, 5).

By making human beings as god, New Agers would drag Jesus down to our level. One of their popular books asserts, "The Son of God . . . is not Jesus but our combined Christ consciousness."

This is derived from basic Hinduism. New Agers may talk a lot about Jesus, but it's not the Jesus we find in the Bible, the unique Lord of creation and humanity's only Saviour. The New Age offers a Hindu counterfeit of Jesus.

Elizabeth Clare Prophet in her book *Lost Years of Jesus* said that Jesus, between the ages of twelve and thirty, traveled to India and studied with Hindu swamis. Some New Agers accuse Christianity of suppressing evidence about Christ's mystical learning in the East. They imagine themselves doing the world a favor now by revealing the real character and teachings of Jesus.

I'd rather believe what the Bible tells us about Jesus, wouldn't you? The Bible says it's only through Jesus that we can come to God. He stands alone as the Way, the Truth, and the Life. This is so essential to our faith that God set up a special appointment week by week for us to worship Jesus Christ as Lord: "The Son of Man is Lord even of the

Sabbath" (Matthew 12:8).

So the Sabbath is the day that reminds us that Jesus Christ is Lord. Week by week on the seventh day He invites our worship, our expression of faith in Him as our Creator and Redeemer. The roots of Sabbath worship go back long before the time of Moses, all the way back to the beginning. On Friday evening of Creation week, the Lord invited Adam and Eve to share the Sabbath celebration of His work.

The seventh-day Sabbath, you see, invites us to commemorate God's work for us as our Creator. And there's another reason we worship God, another reason to keep the seventh day holy.

Come with me reverently to Calvary. It's late Friday afternoon, nearly time to welcome the Sabbath. Jesus, hanging on the cross, recalls all He has done for our salvation. Then with His dying breath He proclaims, "It is finished!" Mission accomplished! Mankind redeemed.

Then our Lord rests on the Sabbath day in honor of His finished work, just as He did after creation. Only this time He rests in the tomb. Following Sabbath rest, Christ arises and ascends to heaven's throne.

Now, the thought of worshiping on Saturday, the seventh-day Sabbath of the fourth commandment, may be new to you. Or you may have heard that Sabbath-keeping is legalistic. Well, nothing could be further from the truth. You see, the word *Sabbath* itself means rest—that's the opposite of works. Each week the Sabbath points us away from our works to rest in God's work for us. And that, my friend, is the gospel!

So every week the Sabbath calls us to honor those twin facts of life, creation and salvation. Let me put it this way. The Sabbath is something like a flag. A nation's flag has no value in itself; it's only special because of what it represents. Even so the Sabbath has no value in itself, except that it represents the greatest things God has done for us, the reasons we worship Him.

Consider this. If the Sabbath had been faithfully remembered by all, there would be no such thing as the New Age heresy.

Honest minds are inquiring, Have we taken Bible truth for granted? Have sincere Christians been confused to the point of cherishing unbiblical beliefs? You may want to do some checking into this matter of Sabbath rest.

Let me tell you the thrilling story of Will Baron. Will was raised in a Christian home, but his search for deeper meaning plunged him into the dungeon of the New Age.

Will got hooked while reading a New Age book about stress. Fascinated, he had to know more. So he visited a psychic fair, where he got acquainted with a channeler. Intrigued, he determined to probe deeper into the occult, attending the Lighted Way metaphysical center in Los Angeles. A woman there channeled the full name of one of Will's friends. Now, Will had never met this woman, and she had never heard about this friend of his. Who but God could communicate such inside information? So Will reasoned.

Fully convinced about the New Age, Will committed himself to the shadowy world of mystical psychology, reincarnation, and other occult concepts. At one point he even spoke in Pentecostal-style tongues. One day while meditating he experienced an incredible visitation from a famous Hindu spirit guide, Djwhal Khul. This majestic being looked just like Jesus as painted by artists. He announced that Will had been chosen to be a special disciple, a priest in training.

Day by day Will received specific instructions from his personal spirit master. He obeyed implicitly, quitting his job as an engineer and moving across the Atlantic to the Findhorn Community in Scotland, a leading New Age center. After six months there the spirit ordered Will to return to the States. He told him where to live and even what car to buy—down to the specific model. Then this spirit being commanded Will to borrow large sums of money for donations to the New Age center.

Nearly bankrupt and emotionally wrecked, Will was a slave of his New Age spirit guide. Then the devil overreached himself. You see, the chief channeler at the center Will attended received orders to transform their group in a New Age "Christian" church. Everyone had to start reading the Bible in order to meet Christians on their own ground and "convert" them to New Age beliefs. Will received special orders from the spirits to infiltrate Christian churches in Los Angeles.

The devil's strategy backfired. There in the Bible, Will met the real Jesus. The Lord of creation and salvation. The Lord of the Sabbath. Rejoicing in his new faith, Will was baptized, and now has a whole new life with God and the assurance of eternal life in Christ. Well, thank God for what He did in Will's life. How about you, my friend? Have you met the real Jesus?

Chapter 6

America's Fading Freedom

Back in seventeenth century Virginia, if you skipped Sunday services, you were in trouble with the law. You lost your food ration for the following week. That was strike one.

If you missed the second Sunday, you forfeited your allowance and were publicly whipped. Strike two. The third week, believe it or not, the law called for you to suffer death. Strike three, and you were out.

Could it possibly be that religious persecution will rear its ugly head here again?

America has deep religious roots, and we are proud of it. Few of us seem concerned that our spiritual roots are riddled with intolerance. A century and a half before our Bill of Rights guaranteed religious liberty, unbelief was a crime. Faith was enforced by law.

In these 1990s, many thoughtful observers of our decade of destiny fear that we are heading back toward religious intolerance. Could this really happen in our land of freedom?

Millions of well-meaning Christians are seeking to save America from immorality through religious

5—D.O.D.

legislation. And I thank God for their interest in morality—not so long ago many ministers taught that the Ten Commandments had been abolished. So we praise the Lord for the current emphasis on moral living—but I'm distressed at the idea of forcing religion upon an unbelieving society. Let's take a look back at colonial history, and I think you will see why.

Back in the seventeenth century, the Puritans came to the New World in search of freedom. They had crossed the Atlantic to escape persecution by the state church of England—only to create another state church of their own. All citizens were required to support the clergy. Magistrates waged war on heresy. Not surprisingly, freedom of conscience suffocated in this medieval-style connection of religion and government.

When William Penn's little band of Quakers sailed past the colony of Massachusetts, they nearly fell prey to a band of Puritan zealots. Listen to this order from Cotton Mather, the famous Puritan clergyman:

> There be now at sea a ship called 'Welcome,' which has on board 100 or more of the heretics and malignants called Quakers. . . . The General Court has given sacred orders to . . . waylay the said 'Welcome' . . . and make captive the said Penn and his ungodly crew, so that the Lord may be glorified and not mocked with the heathen worship of these people. . . . We shall not only do the Lord great good by punishing the wicked, but we shall make great good for His minister and people. Yours in the bowels of Christ, Cotton Mather.

Can you believe it! Thank God, the preacher's

persecuting pirates failed. Penn's Quakers landed safely and with their quiet faith settled Pennsylvania.

The Puritans not only tyrannized others, they oppressed their own citizens. They arrested a sea captain and locked him in the stocks after they spied him kissing his wife on Sunday. One poor man fell into a pond and skipped Sunday services to dry his suit. They whipped him in the name of Jesus. John Lewis and Sarah Chapman, young lovers, were brought to justice for "sitting together on the Lord's day under an apple tree in Goodman Chapman's orchard."

Incredible legalism! And this in a land of freedom?

When Roger Williams first arrived in the Massachusetts Bay Colony, he met a warm welcome. The authorities even invited him to lead Boston's only church, but Williams declined. He could not support the suppression of conscience by government. He knew that most of history's bloody battles have been fought to enforce faith. And all for nothing, since genuine religion cannot be compelled or legislated.

"Magistrates may decide what is due from man to man," Williams said. "But when they attempt to prescribe a man's duties to God, they are out of place." Nothing is more absurd, Williams wrote, than "the setting up of civil power and officers to judge the conviction of men's souls."

Williams also insisted that no citizen should be compelled to support the clergy. "What?" exclaimed the authorities. "Is not the laborer worthy of his hire?" "Yes," Williams replied, "from them that hire him."

Puritan leaders could not tolerate such "new and dangerous opinions." At a formal trial in the year

1635, they condemned Williams and ordered him exiled. And so, banned in Boston, he fled to find refuge with the Indians. "I would rather live with Christian savages," he commented, "than with savage Christians."

Williams purchased property from the Native Americans and established the first modern government offering full freedom of conscience. His settlement at Providence became the blueprint of the American Bill of Rights a century and a half later.

Williams invited all the persecuted and oppressed to find refuge in Providence, whatever their faith. Even if they had no faith, they were welcome. Unfortunately, leaders of Rhode Island who succeeded Williams lapsed into legalism and intolerance, as we shall see later.

History proves that persecution naturally results when faith becomes law. No wonder our national founders had no use for religion by legislation. And neither does God Himself. Jesus put it plainly in Matthew 22:21: "Render therefore to Caesar the things that are Caesar's, and to God the things that are God's."

So things that belong to Caesar—civil government—and things that belong to God—religious matters—must remain separate, lest we return to the days of persecuting patriots.

Have you ever noticed how the Ten Commandments reveal the difference between religious laws and civil laws? They consist of two sections: the first four commandments pertain to one's personal relationship with God. Government cannot enforce them. But the last six commandments—"Thou shalt not kill," for example—are basically civil laws regulating society. These commandments the state must uphold—by whatever means necessary to protect life and property.

When government tampers with religion, problems abound. Consider this matter of school prayer, for example. Naturally our children should lift their hearts in prayer everywhere, including in school.

But who should teach our kids to pray? Do we want Catholic prayers? Protestant prayers? Jewish prayers? Hindu or Muslim prayers? Does it matter?

A while back the California state legislature had a Buddhist chaplain. Many Christians were unhappy about having Buddhist prayers in public schools.

Who gets to choose what to pray? And who gets left out? I think you can see the problem.

Here's a disturbing possibility. Could enforcing school prayer lead to other intrusions into private religion? Perhaps even persecution again? Something to consider carefully.

Now certainly I wish everybody would choose to believe in God and accept biblical morality. But whose interpretation of the Bible? That's the question. Government must protect religion but not promote it.

Again let me emphasize that government ought to enforce civil morality. But here's my concern: Is the pendulum swinging too far now? Will we violate the sacred circle of those first four commandments and interfere with one's personal relationship with God?

Many believe that just so long as government doesn't favor one particular church, all is well. To them, separation of church and state merely forbids a state-sponsored denomination. This may seem reasonable at first—but it's been tried here before with disastrous results.

Consider the Colony of Maryland. It was founded

primarily as a refuge for persecuted Catholics, although Christians of all faiths were welcomed. The Maryland assembly in 1649 proclaimed an "Act of Toleration," which provided that all who confess Jesus shall be welcomed and tolerated. Yet even this so-called "Act of Toleration," as sincere as it was, inspired religious persecution. No liberty was provided for non-Christians. And all who disbelieved a particular doctrine of the Trinity were declared under the death penalty.

Persecution—it naturally results when faith becomes law. Even when nondenominational faith gets enforced. God Himself will not force faith. Why then should we?

Church history from its earliest centuries shows that religious legislation breeds persecution. Back in the year A.D. 321, Roman Emperor Constantine declared Sunday a national day of worship. Eventually Christianity became the official state religion by order of Emperor Theodosius.

Soon the all-powerful church began its persecutions. Anyone who accepted the Bible as the only rule of faith and who insisted upon Jesus alone as intercessor qualified as a heretic. The burning of heretics began at Orleans, France, in 1022. Persecution intensified during the great Crusades. Then came the infamous Inquisition, which slaughtered thousands of Christians, Jews, and Muslims who offended the church.

How could Christians be so cruel? Well, church officials believed that killing heretics saved thousands of others from following them into eternal torment. Even the heretics themselves might repent through fear of the flames. At least that's what church fathers hoped for.

Protestants, while rejecting many medieval traditions, held to the concept of state-sponsored religion. They failed to see that religious legislation is legalism. National salvation by works.

Understanding the meaning of God's day of rest would have preserved Christians from persecuting, from forcing religion upon others.

Force, you see, is quite the opposite of rest. Throughout Christian history ignorance of Sabbath rest has sparked persecution. You recall that the Pharisees plotted to kill Jesus after a dispute about the Sabbath. Later the Christian church, overcome by legalism, persecuted those who would not honor their day of rest.

And, as we saw earlier, Sunday persecution happened in the Protestant American colonies as well. Even Rhode Island after Roger Williams left office passed a Sunday law in 1679 requiring certain acts and forbidding others on the first day of the week. All this for the sake of enforcing Christianity.

But Jesus offers a different solution for the spiritual problems of America. We find His gracious invitation in Matthew 11:28: "Come to Me, all you who labor and are heavy laden, and I will give you rest."

In the passage following this invitation from Christ to come to Him and rest, how appropriate that Jesus reminds us of His day of rest, the day over which He is Lord. Notice: "The Son of Man is Lord even of the Sabbath" (Matthew 12:8).

Jesus Christ is Lord of the Sabbath. Week by week on the seventh day He invites our special expression of faith in Him as our Creator and Redeemer. Had the Sabbath always been kept, there would be no atheism. No godless societies. And no legalism. Sabbath rest—resting in Christ's work for us—helps us to be moral without becoming legalistic.

Let me explain what I mean. In the Ten Commandments, only the Sabbath commandment offers us rest in Christ. The other nine commandments give us work to do. Sabbath rest, you see, provides a foundation of faith for the duties to God and neighbor outlined in the other commandments.

The book of Revelation untangles the mystery of earth's final crisis. In the following passage, immediately before a description of Christ's coming, we find the message God's people will be sharing to the world at the end of time:

> Then I saw another angel flying in the midst of heaven, having the everlasting gospel to preach to those who dwell on the earth—to every nation, tribe, tongue, and people—saying with a loud voice, "Fear God and give glory to Him, for the hour of His judgment has come; and worship Him who made heaven and earth, the sea and springs of water" (Revelation 14:6, 7).

This message God's last-day people proclaim is the everlasting gospel, with a call for the whole earth to worship the Creator in this judgment hour. Creation and salvation through the everlasting gospel—these are the reasons we worship God, our twin facts of life.

Creation and salvation! Is it mere coincidence that these foundations of faith are memorialized by the Sabbath?

Evidently, at the end of time the Sabbath still stands at the foundation of true worship. And how appropriate—in an age of evolution and secular humanism—every week God's Sabbath reminds us that He is our Creator. And with legalism prospering all around us, the Sabbath invites us to rest in

Christ's works for our salvation.

The Bible teaches that God's final test of obedience involves the true faith in Christ versus a legalistic worship. We see this in Revelation 14:12: "Here is the patience of the saints; here are those who keep the commandments of God and the faith of Jesus."

Having faith in Christ and keeping God's commandments! They go together in Sabbath rest.

More and more now, in harmony with the prophecies of Revelation, we see attempts to erode our freedoms. And whenever the power of the state has enforced the goals of the church, personal liberty has been forfeited. Persecution has followed. Remember those old American Sunday laws?

I feel sure of this—when liberty is lost in this country, it won't be because Americans have become bigots and tyrants. No, I'm convinced our freedoms will be voted away, legislated away, amended away by well-meaning Christian patriots who know not what they do. They will sacrifice liberty in a backlash against decades of permissiveness, believing that enforcing religion is America's only hope. Attempting to regain divine favor, they discover too late that they have forged shackles for the soul.

Would you like to know more about this whole question of legislating morality in the light of Bible prophecy? I strongly recommend you read our book *When God Made Rest,* available from the same source from which you received this book. Chapter titles include "When No Man Can Buy or Sell," "Centuries Tell Their Story," "Fingerprints in Stone," "Tyranny of the Crowd." Does it sound interesting? Then be sure to get the book *When God Made Rest.*

It may be during a national crisis of some kind

that our nation will forfeit its freedom. History shows that people in trouble trade off liberty for security. Remember how the Nazis gained power in Germany? And look at the fundamentalism in Iran today. Even here in this country, we could easily exchange some of our freedoms for the sake of economic and military security. Then patriots will persecute in the name of God and country.

As we race toward the crisis hour, we cannot ignore or escape the issues at stake. And our decision must be our own. Satan would like to force his way in. Sometimes even loved ones want to enter—loved ones who do not understand. But God Himself won't violate our freedom to choose. He stands at the door of our heart and knocks. And the honest in heart all over the world will respond to God's call, even at the threat of losing their lives. To these loyal ones Jesus promised, "If you lose your life for My sake, you will save it."

Let me tell you about Noble Alexander, a twentieth-century hero of faith. His government would have left him alone, had he lived his faith silently. But no, the young layman insisted on leading souls to Jesus. So they imprisoned him as a *Plantado*—a rebel against the revolution.

Noble's ordeal began innocently enough. One day the police pulled over his car and politely requested, "Would you mind coming with us to headquarters? We'll only keep you five minutes."

Well, those five minutes turned out to be twenty-two years. More than two decades of suffering I cannot describe. For forty-two days they subjected him to Chinese water torture. Then they starved him for six weeks, demanding that he abandon Jesus Christ. And after Noble refused to work on the Sabbath, they plunged him, with his Adventist friends, into a pool of raw sewage. Four Sabbaths in a row they worshiped God, up to their chins in that slime, singing hymns of praise. Finally the guards let them keep the Sabbath in peace.

Somehow Noble smuggled a Bible into the prison, and every night the prisoners gathered for worship. Catholics, Baptists, Pentecostals, and Adventists prayed and sang together, united by their common faith in Christ.

Noble Alexander remained confined until 1984, when Jesse Jackson negotiated his release and deportation to the United States. Today he works for the Seventh-day Adventist Church in New England.

Recently I had the privilege of meeting Alexander. Let me tell you, after all that man suffered, he is one of the most cheerful, delightful people I've ever met. How thankful he is for America, where he can live for Jesus without fear of the government.

All of us can thank God for the freedoms we enjoy. And when the sad day comes that we lose our freedom, we can still rejoice in the Lord. The same Jesus who sustained Noble Alexander will be with us always, even unto the end—until that glad day when He bursts through the clouds and calls us home. God help us be faithful till that day.

Chapter 7

The 1990s—the End?

Come with me to the Dome of the Rock in Jerusalem. It's one of the most important places on earth for Muslims, Jews, and millions of Christians. Will the Temple Mount upon which the Dome stands be the launching pad for World War III?

No place on earth is more important than the Temple Mount in Jerusalem, site of the golden Dome of the Rock. Muslims, Jews, and millions of Christians have focused their hopes here. And so, in this final chapter of this book, we will consider popular beliefs about Jerusalem and final events on planet Earth.

Why is the Temple Mount so spiritually significant in the minds of millions? Well, the Israelis consider it supremely sacred because their ancestors worshiped here in a sanctuary built by King Solomon.

Then, 600 years before the time of Christ, the Babylonian army destroyed that temple. A second temple replaced it, only to suffer destruction by the Roman army in the year A.D. 70. With that temple destroyed and Jerusalem in ruins, Jewish people scattered all over the world.

Finally, in 1948 Jewish people returned to Palestine to form their new independent government. Then during the dramatic Six-Day War of 1967 they recaptured Jerusalem.

Israelis believe God gave Jerusalem back to them in preparation for building a third temple. After temple services resume, they believe their Messiah will set up His glorious kingdom here. So a rebuilt temple on this Mount would fulfill the dreams of Jewish people everywhere.

Now, how does Christianity get involved? Well, many sincere Christians also anticipate a new temple in Jerusalem. To them, Bible prophecy requires the rebuilding of a Jewish temple here. This will set the stage for Christ to come in triumph and rule the world. That's according to their belief, of course.

So millions of Christians join Jewish people in expecting a restoration of temple services in Jerusalem. There's just one problem, and it's a big one. The Temple Mount is under Muslim control, and the Dome of the Rock remains one of Islam's holiest shrines. You see, Abraham (whom they call "Ibrahim") offered his son to God (whom they call "Allah") on the sacred rock underneath the dome. Muslims also believe their pioneer Muhammad, whom they honor as their prophet, ascended to heaven from that same rock. No wonder Arabs everywhere would spill their last drop of blood to prevent the Israelis from erecting a temple there.

Jewish people, in turn, consider the present Muslim occupation of the Temple Mount an unspeakable outrage. The ancient temple on this site contained the Holy of Holies. Nobody could set foot there except the high priest once a year. You see why Muslim possession of the Temple Mount is an intolerable abomination, as far as the Israelis are concerned.

It's a no-win situation. Both Jews and Muslims claim divine rights to the Temple Mount. Somebody gets desecrated no matter what happens here.

Well, what will happen in Jerusalem? Does Bible prophecy offer any clues?

Chuck Colson, a key Watergate figure and now a committed Christian, recently wrote a compelling book *Kingdoms in Conflict.* He proposes a chain of events centered around Jerusalem's Dome of the Rock, problems that pull the superpowers into earth's final crisis.

Let's take a look at Chuck Colson's spine-chilling scenario. It takes place in the year 1998. Please understand that he is not suggesting the end of the world has to happen at that time or in that particular way. But his portrayal will help us understand the kind of international incident many of our fellow Christians fervently look forward to.

The end-time crisis in Jerusalem begins innocently enough. Israel's rival political groups, the Labor and the Likud parties, find themselves engaged in yet another power struggle. Both parties negotiate with splinter groups, seeking to patch together a majority coalition and gain control of the government.

A breakthrough appears likely when the Likud party links up with the Tehiya, a small but significant group of religious zealots. The Tehiya promises to deliver the votes the Likud needs, for a price. They want to blow up the Muslims' Dome of the Rock while the government looks the other way. Then they will make their move in rebuilding the Jewish temple.

Now the White House gets wind of the secret negotiations between the Likud and the Tehiya.

Armed with a CIA report of the secret deal shaping up, our President summons his top cabinet members and military advisors for an urgent council.

"Gentlemen," he begins, "sorry to call you in so early this morning. We seem to have a little trouble brewing in Israel. You all know that the Knesset has been paralyzed for some time. But this morning's intelligence summary suggests that the logjam between the Likud and the Labor parties is beginning to break." He proceeds to explain what the Likud and the Tehiya groups are getting ready to do.

At the President's direction, the national security advisor explains about the Tehiya group. Some big industrialists in Israel finance them, along with a Christian fundamentalist group in Texas.

The Tehiya believe that the Arab-Israeli standoff can be solved only by violence. After they blow up the Muslim Dome, they plan to move so fast the Arabs will not have time to react. They already have marble slabs precut for rebuilding the temple. And they have men in training—not only commandos, but priests. Priests learning to perform Jewish sacrificial rites.

Priests? Sacrificial rites? The President's advisors scratch their heads in disbelief. But they know what to do. One way or another, they must stop the Israelis. If the Dome of the Rock is destroyed, Muslim nations will unite, and war will break out in the Middle East. The Soviets might move in to help their Arab allies. That would mean a showdown with the United States and possible nuclear war.

No question about it; the Israelis must be stopped.

Our President agrees with his advisors' political wisdom. He senses his responsibility to nip the Israeli plan in the bud. Persuade them, threaten them, even use military force to protect the Dome—anything to prevent a possible World War III.

But the President hesitates. You see, his religious beliefs conflict with his political and military instincts. All his life he's been looking forward to the rebuilding of the Jewish temple in Jerusalem. That's his blessed hope. Now that his dream is coming true, how can he snuff it out?

The President tries to explain his convictions to his perplexed advisors. Picking up a well-worn leather Bible from his desk, he tells them earnestly, "God's Word predicts the rebuilding of the Jewish temple in Jerusalem. I ran my campaign on the Bible, and I intend to run this nation by the Scriptures. As for me, I will never lift my hand against God's chosen people. Let's keep in mind while we make our plans that God has already made His." He then concludes the meeting with prayer.

Please remember that Colson is not suggesting that the end of the world has to happen in any particular way. But Colson helps us understand the events many Christians fervently anticipate. I have doubts about their interpretations that I will explain in a few pages.

The American President attempts to contact the Israeli government to discuss the crisis. They ignore him. They well understand his beliefs about Bible prophecy, and they determine to take advantage of him in achieving their political goals.

That evening the President phones a trusted friend, the dean of a Bible college, to discuss the crisis in Israel. Let's pick up the conversation as the President exclaims: "Slow down, if you don't mind. I'm taking notes. The first principle, then, is that we must stand with the Jews. No matter what."

The President jots it all down on a yellow legal pad propped against his knee. "And it makes no difference whether the Israeli government believes in God or whether they're non-believing nationalists. The point is that Israel today is the biblical nation with the rebuilt temple to which Jesus returns."

The President continues his scribbling. "Yes, I think I know all that pretty well. The rapture and the tribulation—and yes, Armageddon. Which would be just about the end of the story—as far as these events are concerned."

The President beams with joy. "Dean, I can't tell you how much you have helped me. I'm familiar with all this from my own reading and Bible study, of course, but you've given me a succinct summary.

"Pray that God will give me wisdom. God bless you."

As the President hangs up the phone, his chief of staff, who overheard the conversation, jumps in with an unsolicited warning:

"Mr. President, you're scaring me to death! You're responsible for hundreds of millions of lives, including mine, including my wife and kids. And you seem to be guiding us by some obscure, strange theory about the end of the world. Americans elected you because you were moral and upright, have one wife, nice kids, and speak soothingly on TV. You can't betray their trust! Surely God did not put you in the White House to cheer on the Israelis while they blunder into World War III. We have to make a military move now to seal off the Temple Mount—or there will be war."

"No!" the President shouts. "I will never lift a

hand against God's chosen people."

The next morning it happens. The national security advisor bursts in with the news: "Mr. President! The Dome of the Rock has been destroyed! One minute ago Israeli commandos blew it up. Hundreds of casualties."

For a moment the President stands speechless. The grim-faced advisor continues: "I think we'd better get the Soviet leader on the phone."

The President nods and turns to his desk. Over the Oval Office television, the Christian channel triumphantly airs the "Battle Hymn of the Republic"—"Glory, glory Hallelujah! His truth is marching on!"

Well, that's the spine-tingling scenario proposed by some Christians. What do you think? More important, what does the Bible have to say? Until recently, such a situation would have seemed impossible—a sensible, moral leader letting the world slip to the brink of Armageddon! But now such circumstances loom as a disturbing possibility. And if this nightmare comes true, millions of Christians would welcome it as the signal of Christ's glorious return.

Is this a true picture of last-day events, according to the Bible? There's so much for me to tell and so little space here. We do have a book, *Showdown at Armageddon,* that explains all my convictions about Jerusalem and Bible prophecy. Some of the chapter titles are "Antichrist's Civil War," "Secret of the Rapture," and "Counterfeiting Armageddon." *Showdown at Armageddon* is available from the same source from which you got this book you are reading.

Now let me open my heart about Jerusalem and Bible prophecy. I'm deeply concerned about making a rebuilt Jewish temple the center of spiritual revival. Hal Lindsey, in his book *The Late Great Planet Earth*, predicts that "there will be a reinstitution of the Jewish worship according to the law of Moses with sacrifices and oblations" (p. 46).

Can you imagine that—modern animal sacrifices in Jerusalem! Wouldn't such an abomination compete with Calvary and deny the saving sacrifice of our Lord Jesus Christ?

You recall that when Jesus died, the veil of the temple tore apart, symbolizing the end of Jewish temple services and sacrifices.

Restoring those animal sacrifices would contradict what Christ has accomplished as the Lamb of God. And there's a word for that, it's *blasphemy.*

Never forget it, friend. Anything that competes with the finished sacrifice of Christ is the work of Satan. So how can we hope and pray that Jerusalem's temple will be rebuilt, anticipating that animal sacrifices will be offered on its altar? How could we consider such idolatry a spiritual revival?

I think you will agree that we are raising important questions here. Questions that deeply concern anyone who appreciates Calvary as the complete and only sacrifice for sin.

And what about this notion of Israel's being God's chosen nation?

Notice what the Bible says in Galatians 3:9, 29: "So then those who are of faith are blessed with believing Abraham." "If you are Christ's, then you are Abraham's seed, and heirs according to the promise."

According to the Bible, only those who are Christ's are children of Abraham and heirs of the covenant promises. Enlightened Bible scholars know that the Old Testament is not primarily Israel-centered, but Messiah-centered. And the New Testament points us away from any Jewish temple on earth to heaven's sanctuary, where Jesus intercedes for us. Notice:

Now this is the main point of the things we are saying: We have such a High Priest, who is seated at the right hand of the throne of the Majesty in the heavens, a Minister of the sanctuary and of the true tabernacle which the Lord erected, and not man" (Hebrews 8:1, 2).

Evidently God's true temple is in heaven now. The Lord built it, not man. Anything we could build down here would be a counterfeit temple. And that which glorifies the work of man in building such a false temple must be false teaching.

Nothing could be more clear than this: True prophecy points upward to heaven's temple in the New Jerusalem, while false prophecy points downward to an earthly temple in old Jerusalem.

All this talk about rebuilding the Jewish temple down here—are we setting ourselves up for a counterfeit Armageddon? You know Jesus warned about false prophets with their false predictions concerning His coming. Could it be that all the attention showered upon Israel is a smoke screen of the enemy? An attempt to divert sincere Christians from the real issues of Armageddon?

And now, as we near the end of these pages, I'm thinking of all the explosive issues we've discussed, the compelling problems of our decade of destiny: AIDS, fragmenting families, deadly addictions, crime, and homelessness—there is no human solution to all this heartache. Our only hope is God's blessed hope, the soon coming of our Lord and Saviour Jesus Christ. Nobody knows just when the Lord Jesus will burst through the clouds and call us home. But based on rapidly fulfilling Bible prophecy, I can assure you, that glorious day is coming soon.

Praise God, Jesus is coming soon! And He's coming to take us up to His heavenly home.

Some years ago a boy quarreled with his father and left home. His parting words were bitter and rebellious: "You'll never see me again!"

Three years passed—three tough years. He wanted to go home, but he was afraid. Would his father let him come back? He wrote his mother, told her that he would be on a certain train as it passed the house. He asked her to hang something white in the yard if it was all right with his dad to come home.

The boy was nervous on the train—sat in one seat and then another. A minister noticed and asked what was wrong. He told him. They rode along together as the boy looked out the window.

Suddenly the boy jumped up excitedly. "Look, sir, my house is just around the bend. Will you please look for me, please see if there is something white? I can't stand to look myself."

The train lurched as it rounded a slow curve. The minister kept his eyes focused. Then, forgetting his dignity, he shouted, "Look, son, look!"

There was the little farmhouse under the trees. But you could hardly see the house for the white. It seemed that those lonely parents had taken every white sheet in the house, every bedspread, every tablecloth, even every handkerchief—everything they could find that was white—and hung them out on the clothesline and on the trees!

The boy stared blankly. His lips quivered. Before the train had completely stopped at the water tank, he jumped out. The last the minister saw of him, he was running up the hill as fast as his legs could carry him—toward the sheets fluttering in the wind, toward home!

That's how God feels about you, my friend. He yearns for you to come home!

I like to picture that great homecoming day. What a procession it will be, with Jesus Himself leading the way! With harps and crowns and songs of delight. In God's glorious eternity there will be no homelessness, no pollution, no prisons or hospitals. No heart will ever break. No voice will ever say goodbye.

I want to be there, and I know you do too. I urge you to make your reservation just now.